Amani

Wants to Fly

Other books by Barry Mann

Miri and her Drum Set

Amani
wants to *Fly*

Barry Mann

Illustrations by Meira Ner-David

Dragonfeather Books
Bedazzled Ink Publishing Company • Fairfield, California

paperback 978-1-960373-49-6

Cover Artwork
by
Meira Ner-David

Cover Design
by

Sapling Studio

Dragonfeather Books
Bink Books
a division of
Bedazzled Ink Publishing, LLC
Fairfield, California
http://www.bedazzledink.com

I am the real-life Amani. Her story is my story.

When I was two years old, I overheard my parents say that they were relieved not to have to worry about my becoming a pilot when I was older because I always fell asleep in the back of a moving vehicle. In that moment, I decided that I would learn to fly when I grew up. The truth was, I felt comfortable and happy in the back of a moving vehicle, and that was why I slept so well back there.

As I got older, I enjoyed playing video games. I got a lot of practice, and I was pretty good at them. My dad once said to me, as he watched me with the controls, "With that hand eye coordination you should take flying lessons." I was elated to hear him say that.

For my twelfth birthday, I begged for those flying lessons to begin. One of my dad's friends took me up for my first lesson in a small plane. I felt free, peaceful, and empowered, all at the same time. My parents said that as long as I kept my grades up and always tried my best, I could take one lesson a week.

I LOVED my flying lessons. Some kids at school thought it was cool that I was learning to fly, but others thought it was strange. Some made fun of me. Some grownups discouraged me, too, saying that flying was too dangerous a thing to do, especially for a girl. But others, like my parents and Charles "Pete" Conrad Jr—the third man to walk on the moon—told me I could do anything I chose to do, as long as I kept up my hard work, dedication, and positive attitude.

I now fly the heavy Boeing 787 internationally for a major US Airline, and I love my job and the people I get to work with. I'm so glad that I followed my passion and trusted the adults who supported me along the way.

JoAnna Marmon
Pilot

Dedicated to all parents who encourage their children to be what they want to be

Amani lives with her mother and father in the city of Philadelphia.

When Amani was small, her father would push her on the swing.
"Push me higher, Daddy, higher—to the moon!"

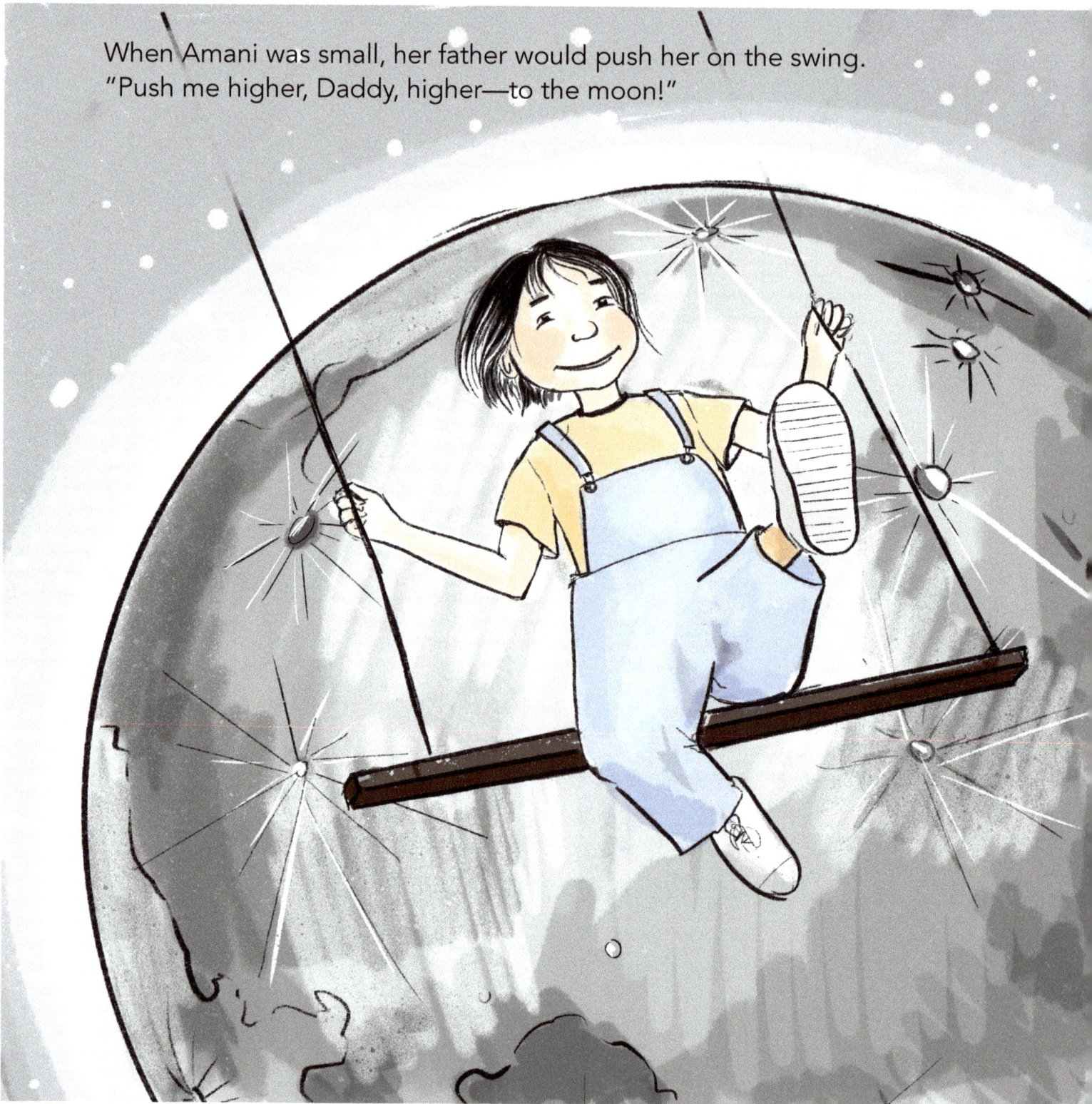

Whenever Amani's father flew across the ocean, she and her mother went to the airport to watch the planes.

At the library, Amani always found books about flying.

In her reading class, Amani gave an oral report about the Wright Brothers who were American aviation pioneers.

"Someday I would like to be a pilot," said Amani.
A boy in her class laughed and shouted, "Girls can't be pilots."

Amani's teacher told the boy his words were incorrect and impolite.

When Amani told her parents what the boy in her class said, her father took her to the library to read about Amelia Earhart, the first female to fly solo across the Atlantic Ocean.

"You can be whatever you want to be," her father told her.

In high school, Amani was most interested in mathematics and the science of weather.

One day Amani taught her class about the forces that allow a plane to fly: Lift, Weight, Thrust, and Drag.

In high school, Amani got a job at a flight school after school and on weekends.

For pay, the school gave her free flying lessons!

By the time she graduated from high school, Amani had enough hours to fly by herself in a small plane.

The next year, Amani became an instructor.

In college Amani studied aeronautical engineering (how a plane flies).
"There is a lot to learn!"

Soon Amani was trained to fly big planes that take hundreds of passengers on long trips.

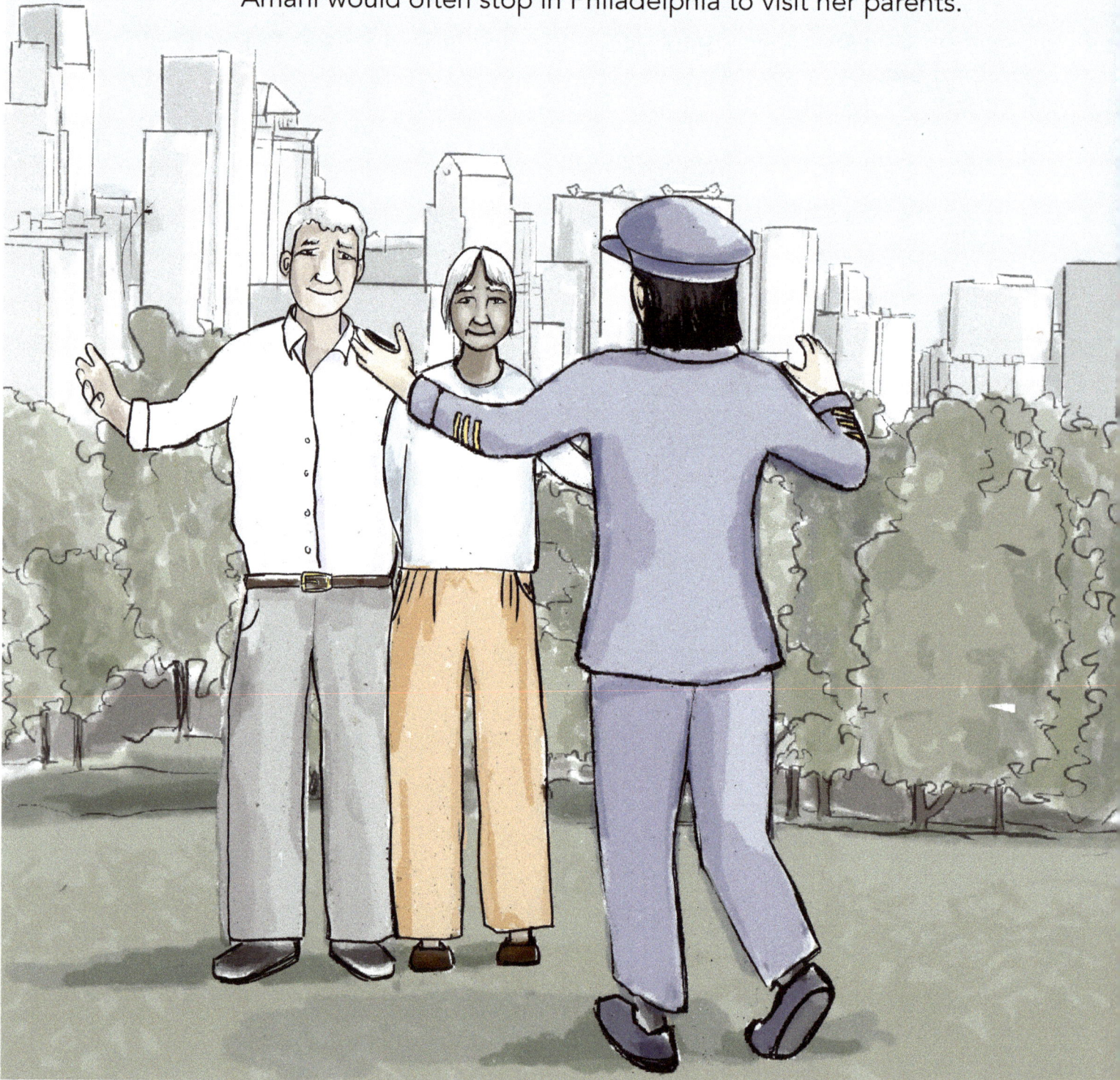

Amani would often stop in Philadelphia to visit her parents.

Amani invited her father to fly with her when he needed to go across the ocean.

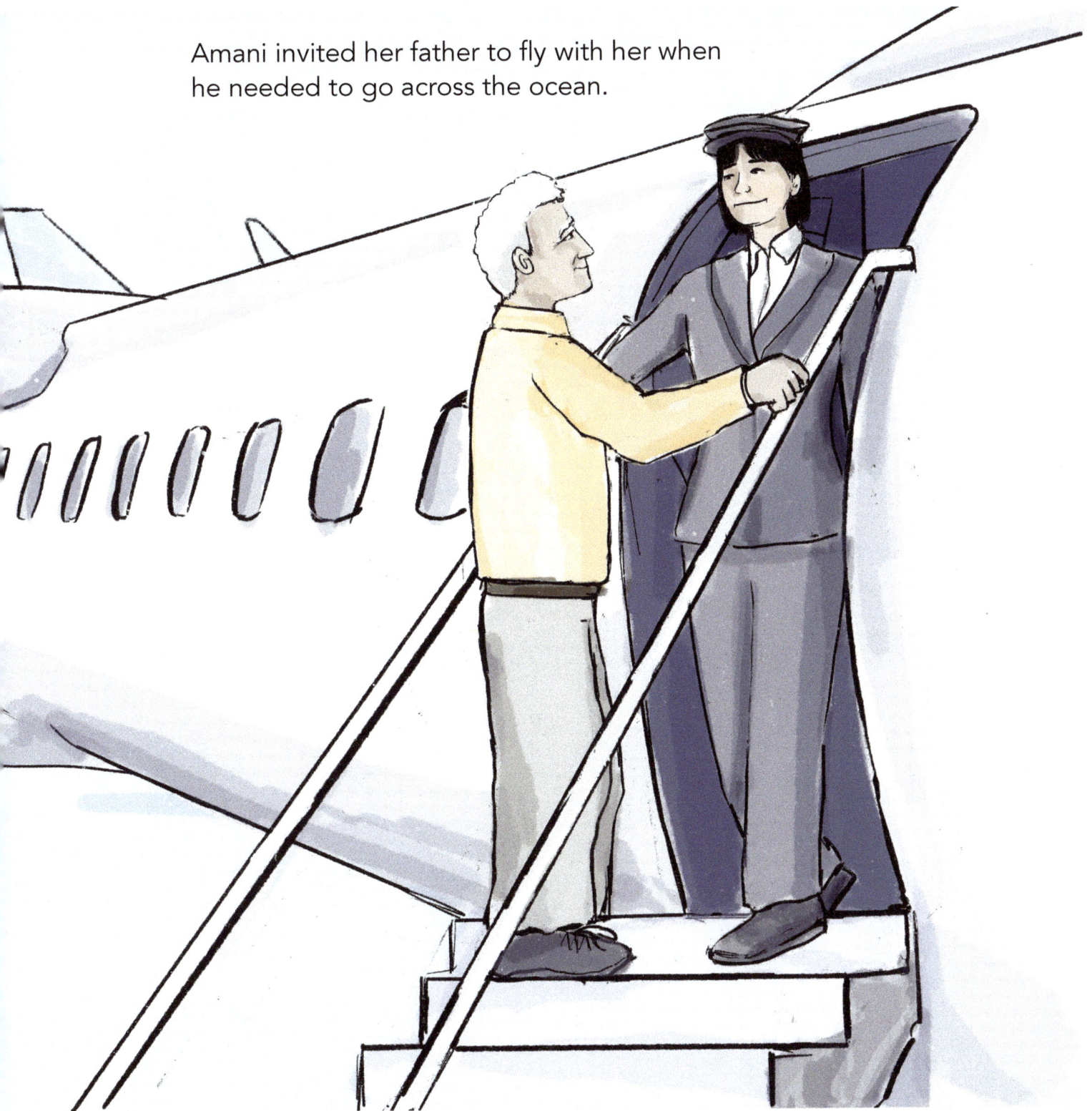

Amani's father heard her voice from the cockpit: "Good morning, passengers, and welcome aboard! I promise you a safe and smooth flight—especially since my father is also a passenger today."

He was so proud seeing his daughter living her dream.

The Four Forces of Flight

LIFT

DRAG

THRUST

WEIGHT

Lift
The force created by the wings and by the air hitting the underside of the wings, that keeps an airplane in the air.

Weight
The force of gravity that pulls the aircraft towards the ground.

Thrust
The force moving the aircraft forward along its flight path.

Drag
The total aerodynamic force that opposes the aircraft's motion through the air.

Altitude
Location in the sky relative to sea level

Air Speed
Speed of the aircraft through the air

Attitude
The angle measured between the airplane's path and the horizon

Horizon
The horizon is the line at which the earth's surface and the sky appear to meet

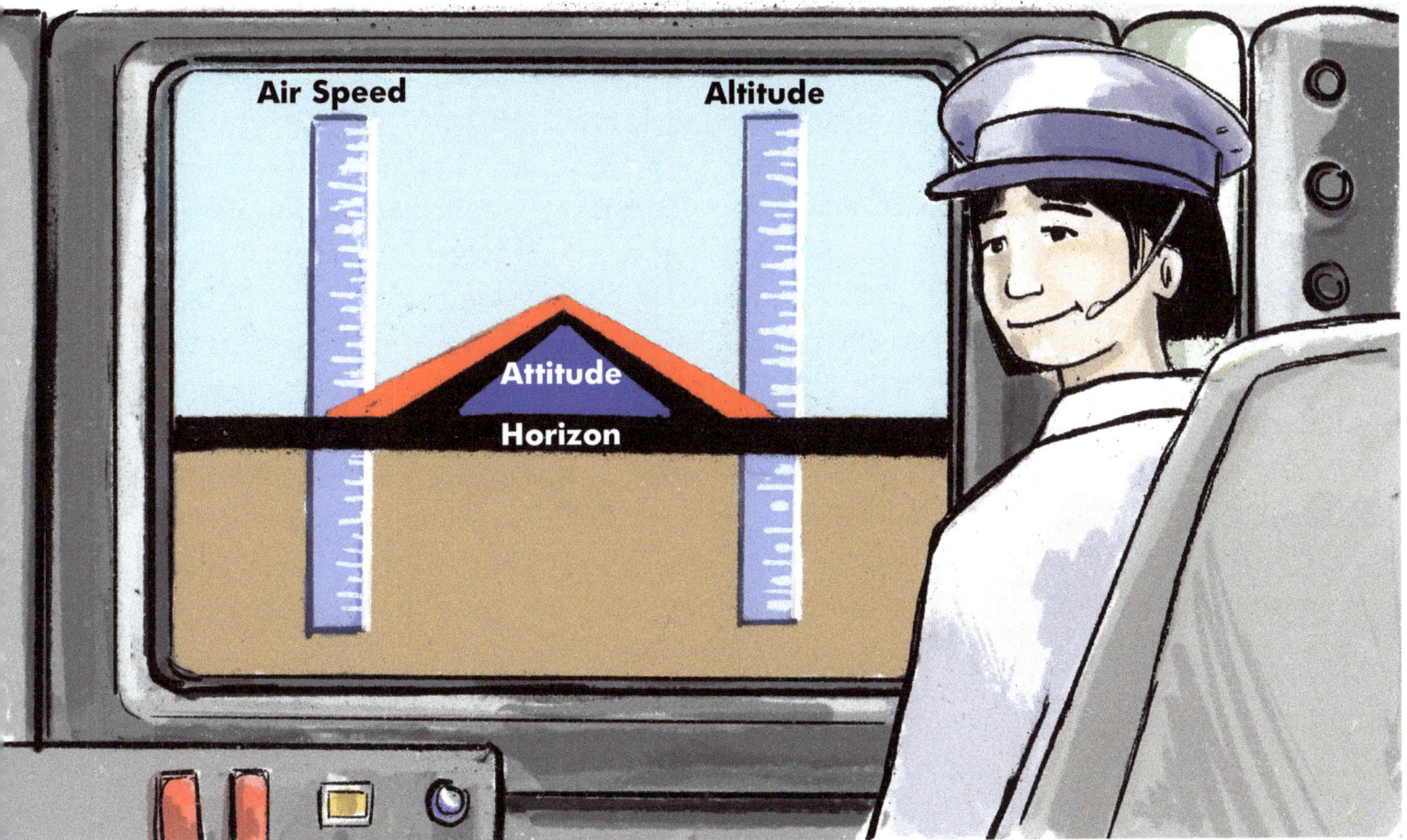

JoAnna Marmon was born and raised in Philadelphia, Pennsylvania. As a teenager, she worked behind the front counter at Hortman Aviation Services flight school in return for flying lessons, and by the time she graduated from high school, she had earned her Private Pilot's License, her Instrument Rating, and her Commercial License. She went on to study at the University of Pennsylvania, majoring in Spanish and graduating one class shy of minors in Math, Physics, and Astronomy. She earned her Certified Flight Instructor Rating while in college.

JoAnna reached 1500 hours of flight time while flight instructing for Hortman Aviation at Northeast Philadelphia Airport. She then flew CRJ 200s for a US regional airline and was part of the team founding the space tourism startup called Ion Space Expeditions (ISE). She was hired by a major US airline in 2017 and started flying their Airbus 320 fleet. In 2018, she transitioned to flying the BOEING 757 and BOEING 767 and began flying passengers to Europe for the first time in her career. She now flies the BOEING 787 primarily between the USA and Europe.

During the COVID-19 pandemic, JoAnna became a mom and took a leave of absence to be with her family and to work on projects from home, including starting a flight school with her husband. It's called Beyond Aviation Flight School, and it's located at the South Jersey Regional Airport in Lumberton, NJ and at the Atlantic City International Airport, also in NJ.

Barry Mann is a retired surgeon and currently the System Medical Director for Health Equity in the Main Line Health System of suburban Philadelphia, where he previously served as Chief Academic Officer and director of the surgical residency training program. Dr. Mann has received numerous prestigious awards for his work in medical education, including the Distinguished Teacher of Medicine Award from the American Association for Medical Colleges, and the Distinguished Educator Award from the Association for Surgical Education. While professor of surgery at the Sidney Kimmel Medical College of Thomas Jefferson University in Philadelphia, he co-authored five medical textbooks including *SURGERY: A Competency Based Companion*.

Amani Wants to Fly is his second children's book. It was inspired by his continuing commitment to reducing gender inequality in the workplace, and by parents who encourage their children to be what they want to be. His first children's book, *Miri and her Drum Set*, celebrates the shared values and vocabulary that unite people across religions and cultures.

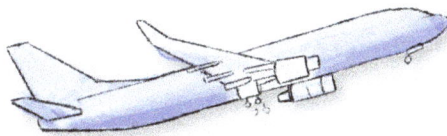

Meira Ner-David is currently a student of architecture at the Bezalel Academy of Arts and Design in Jerusalem, Israel, and is also a painter and an illustrator. She has illustrated the children's books *Yonah and the Mikveh Fish* and *Miri and her Drum Set*, and created the cover art for several novels including *Hope Valley*, *Dreaming Against the Current*, and *To Die in Secret*.

www.ingramcontent.com/pod-product-compliance
Lightning Source LLC
Chambersburg PA
CBHW061413090426

42741CB00023B/3496